CHANGE MANAGEMENT

CHANGE MANAGEMENT

New Words for Old Ideas

Garth Holloway

To order additional copies of this book, contact:
Xlibris LLC
1-800-455-039
www.xlibris.com.au
Orders@xlibris.com.au
521983

Acknowledgements

With thanks to:
Shamim Ur Rashid for the cover design;
Victor-Adrain Cruceanu for the graphics;
Stephany Aulenback for editing the book;
Charles, Kailash, and Venkatesh for their friendship; and Russell Swanborough
for informing so much of my foundation thinking; and finally
Amit Kumar Das for his unbelievable inspiration.

Dedication

To my late father with all my love.

Contents

Preface

Thank you for taking the time to read some or all of the articles contained in this collection.

This is the second in a series of three books. The first book is a collection of longer articles on a selection of the common business concepts that a manager may be expected to encounter throughout the various stages of their career and the third provides a range of tools and techniques for the manager's kitbag.

The purpose of the book is to consolidate and capture my thoughts on the many facets of change management.

The articles are not intended to provide detailed instructions or methodology on how to apply each concept. Rather the intent is to provide enough detail to convey the essence of the concepts, sufficient for the reader to apply them in their own business without the rigidity of an instruction manual.

As each paper is written as a stand-alone article, a number of the central concepts are repeated in the different papers. This has been kept to a minimum but could not be completely avoided.

Why Change Needs Politically Incorrect Managers

The leadership of transformational change has to be one of the most difficult disciplines a manager can master. For me, the biggest hurdle is the capacity of managers to be unreasonable for a sustained amount of time.

"If you argue with a fool, they will drag you down to their level and beat you with experience." Anonymous.

Having worked in the discipline of change for over twenty years I have learnt a few things:

1. 80% is frequently considered good enough.
2. Consultants need to be forced out of their comfort zones.
3. Sponsorship is a misunderstood role.
4. A project is always stronger when there is a person who is willing to be politically incorrect.

As a consultant, it is not difficult to lead the thinking at a client site. This is almost what you get paid for. But despite all the intellectual property a consulting firm has in the "cupboard," the thought leadership provided by a consultant is frequently no better than the sum of their experiences. And because the client does not really know better, this leadership is treated as appropriate for the project at hand.

The most frequently used consulting approach is to rely on experience and the deliverables previously prepared for somebody else on a different project. This material gets reworked, refreshed, re-presented and re-invoiced. Nothing fundamentally wrong with this as it is part of the value that consultants offer.

At this point in the project the client is impressed. They have a concept deliverable they can review and critique. The relationship is working well. But here's the problem. The client's thinking becomes constrained by the tabled deliverable. They start to critique what's there. The far more powerful critique of "what's not there" is often missed.

Then the client is faced with a problem. How do they tell the consultant what they have produced is just rubbish? Not only is it rubbish, but they don't want to pay for it either. Managers tend to be diplomatic and in the intimacy of a consulting engagement they don't want to fracture the relationship. So they ask the consultant for changes and refinements and so start down the journey of accepting 80% of what they really wanted in the first place.

When the consultant runs up against a client who knows their own mind and who has a clear picture of the deliverable, then the consultant is forced to raise their game. No longer can they provide clever ideas on PowerPoint that could mean more than one thing depending on how the conversation goes.

But to find a client who knows their own mind is rare. Sure, every manager will say, "I am my own person." This is true at a private or small group level, but less so in the public forum of meetings and written communications. In these arenas the manager becomes diplomatic and couches the message. This happens for a few reasons:

1. They are unsure of what the answer should be. They know what the consultant provided is wrong, but cannot easily explain why.
2. Their colleagues seem to be happy, so the manager starts to believe they don't get it. They must be missing something.

3. If the manager speaks out and causes the project to change and then it turns out they were wrong, it could be embarrassing or career-limiting.

4. The project brief was given by more senior managers and the manager does not believe they have the authority or insight required to change the course of the project. If the project was off track, surely the senior manager would have done something about it.

It is unlikely that these four points can ever be fully mitigated and a certain diplomacy is needed, otherwise the project will never deliver anything. But the primary mitigation is to ensure the sponsor is strong and willing to be unreasonable. As long as they are willing to tell the project team that the deliverables are unacceptable and to minimise any compromise from this position, then the project will remain healthy.

I quite like the advertisement for Nissan. It shows the product development team presenting the latest features to the senior executive. They are excited about what they have produced. He just looks at them and says, "More." No discussion. Just do better. Eventually they produce an output that works for the executive. They present the price. He says, "Less."

It's a great example of being unreasonable. Drive the team to get what you want. Anything less is to accept a deliverable that is only 80% complete.

I once listened to a long presentation by a senior manager. At the end he asked if I agreed. I said, "I agree with 98% of what you've said." His response was excellent. Basically it went: to hell with the 98%! The 2% is the bit of value.

This incident has stuck with me for nearly 20 years. The 2% is the only bit of value. The same applies to projects. It is not hard to get 80% complete. It is very hard to get 100% complete. But because 80% looks like a lot, it is accepted and the last 20%—the bit with the real value, the bit that changes the project from adequate to exceptional—is poorly delivered.

The hard reality is that it will take almost the same effort to realise the value in the last 20% as it did to produce the first 80%. Finishing anything always takes longer than expected and projects are no different. The sponsor is now also up against change fatigue, boredom and indifference from the project team and the subject matter experts who have been involved in the project. By now these people are "over it" and they just want it to finish. They will have a hundred reasons why close enough is good enough.

This is where the sponsor needs to be very strong and uncompromising. Drive the value out from this last 20%.

From the consultant's point of view, they have spent their time chasing the 80% and the budget is almost fully consumed. They realise that delivering the 20% could lead to free consulting. They need to avoid this so they start to push a narrative that says the 80% was in fact the scope of the project and the 20% is extra. Chances are they even have a scope document that supports this position. The problem is that they articulated the 100% vision to the client but sold the 80% deliverable. They sold the augmented business benefit—the benefit the client could get if they did five other things to improve their business over and above buying the consultant's solution. It is not an easy game. The client would not have bought the solution if they knew they needed to do the other five things as well. The consultant knows that their solution will deliver value to the client and that the client just doesn't get it yet. They are confident that by the end of the project the client will see the value and be glad of the project. So the consultant sells the client what they are willing to buy and figures that they will work out the details later. This is all good until the project budget runs out. This brings us around full circle—the sponsor needs to be very strong and uncompromising. Hold the consultancy to account. "Give me the value you promised."

A feature of the last 20% is that it is likely to comprise the intangible deliverables of the project. It represents the answer to the question of "so what?" The 80% project delivered an ERP solution—so what? The 80% delivered re-engineered processes—so what? Can the sponsor bank the benefit?

The role of the sponsor is to define the project and accept the deliverables and in my opinion to be absolutely dogmatic on ensuring the deliverables produce the bankable outcomes and benefits described at the start. But if it was easy, everybody would be doing it.

Why Entrepreneurs Need To Take Baths

Entrepreneurship—the act and art of being an entrepreneur (Source: Wikipedia).

When I was growing up my father told me a lot of things. Most of it passed me by as I already thought I knew everything there was to know on the subject or because it was my father telling me. There were however, two messages that stuck and have remained in the forefront of my mind throughout my professional life.

The first was the story of how he came to run his own business. Basically it went like this:

"I used to come home at night and lie in the bath and think about the problems I was dealing with at work. One day I realised that it was my bath and if I was going to worry about anyone's problems while I was in my own bath, then they should be mine. While I was worrying about my company's problems, I wasn't worrying about my own."

Based on this realisation he quit his job.

He went on to say:

"Nothing gets you focused on your own problems like having two young kids and no income. Now when I lie in my bath at night I worry about my own problems and how I am building a life for my family."

He tried real estate sales and a couple of other ventures. Then he met a chap who had some great software but no sales. Together they built a successful software services business and he retired with peace of mind that he had looked after his family.

Over the years, there were a few variations on this story and each time he would conclude with the assertion: "When you lie in your bath at night, make sure you know whose problems you are thinking of."

The second message he left me with was that the word "creative" lacked a second "c." That the word really should be "creaCtive"—a combination of the words "active" and "creative." There is no point in being creative if you do not act on your thoughts.

I consider these two bits of wisdom to be some of the best I have ever received.

The message is simple for would-be self-employed entrepreneurs—worry about your own problems and do something about them.

For the internal entrepreneur it gets a bit more complex. Bath time becomes the time when the manager steps back from the desk and actively considers how the function they are managing contributes to the overall business. Bath time is the time needed to reflect and look for the insights that other people are not seeing. It is about looking at problems from different angles.

It is very easy and somewhat lazy to let the routine of day-to-day business suck you in and to allow yourself to be controlled by your diary. When I ask managers to show me the documents they use to manage their business process, they frequently refer me to their diary. A diary manages time, not the business. How often do you say or hear, "I don't have time to think." Does this mean that you don't have time to actively evaluate your contribution to the business?

Without making time to work on the business, managers can find themselves moving from meeting to meeting, having significant discussions but not necessarily achieving much. This is where "creactivity" must meet entrepreneurialism. You cannot be entrepreneurial without action. You cannot be entrepreneurial and stay in the crowd.

As an employee, acting on your ideas is difficult. It is likely that a manager does not have the mandate to implement big ideas (as opposed to incremental change) and "making it happen" will require an enormous amount of "creactivity." Change management becomes vital for success. In this instance I define change management as the internal socialisation and lobbying of the idea. As a self-employed manager, you are entitled to implement whatever decision you choose. As an employed manager, you need the support of the senior executives or directors.

To be successful as an internal entrepreneur requires that the manager is very clear on the answer to the question, "Am I addressing a symptom or a primary issue?"

But how do you know? If you are not part of the senior leadership team you may not be privy to the more fundamental issues facing the company. In this case you need to be equally clear on the following change management questions:

- Who will support the idea for implementation?
- Who will take responsibility for the activity?
- What does success look like?
- Who will gain from the experience?
- Who will own the risk?

Being clear on the answers to these questions will significantly improve the way you communicate and market the idea within the company. You may ask yourself, "Why should I bother? I have a good idea and if the company is not interested, then that's the company's problem, not mine."

Being an entrepreneur is not easy. If you are happy being a good employee, then turn up every day and do a professional job. Write your ideas down in an email and move on. If you want more, if you want to make a big contribution to the growth of the company, then you need to look at the business as if it were your own and take time to think about the big picture. Bath time is a good time to do this. So is mowing the lawn or any other time when you can be alone with your thoughts.

How do you start? Draw a picture; write up a mock marketing brochure. Not a PowerPoint slide pack, but a proper A4 brochure that describes your idea. Keep it to one page. It is not a technical document. It's a marketing document. If you can express your idea on one page and include a picture, then you are well on your way to making a great start to commercialising your idea.

Managing Risk,
A Trigger For Change

Having spent considerable time on business transformation projects, I can say with a high degree of confidence that the discipline of change management is becoming so watered down it is at risk of becoming more of a catchphrase than a serious discipline. The term is bandied about freely whenever a project is discussed without any real thought of what it will mean for the project. When project concerns are raised, the response is frequently along the lines of, "That's a change management issue" or 'We will ask the change manager to deal with that."

The upshot is, for any given project, change management is treated as a catchall. Having said that, in many respects, this position is in fact acceptable, as the primary deliverable from almost every project is a change in behaviour at the individual and collective level.

The question for each project therefore becomes, then, how do you create a common understanding of what change management means for that specific project?

Recently I was asked to prepare a project initiation document (PID) for a client, working off their template. The template included all the standard headers such as objectives, scope, risk management, change management, budget and timeline.

This got me turning over an old chestnut of mine: what's the difference between risk and change management?

My view is that the major reason to employ a change manager on any project is to mitigate risk and the biggest risks on any project are those represented by stakeholder behaviour. This includes scenarios where stakeholders:

1. Do not embrace the need for the project.
2. Do not accept the deliverables of the project.
3. Cannot / will not work with the deliverables of the project.

Consider the last PID or Statement of Work (SOW) you prepared or read. It probably had a risk section with a structure and text similar to this one.

Risk Description	Likelihood	Impact	Mitigation Strategy
Misaligned goals			Prepare and socialise a detailed project definition document
Poor communication of objectives			Prepare and socialise a detailed project definition document
Resistance to change			Administer an enlistment program
Insufficient budget			Prepare and socialise a detailed project definition document
			Use document to prepare project investment estimate
			Apply a 20% risk loading
Insufficient resource allocation			Prepare and socialise a detailed project definition document
			Confirm allocation of resources
Expectation to eliminate duplicate records not realised			Engage all relevant stakeholders and ensure requirements sign off
			Engage sites and branches around process
Key stakeholders outside shared services reject solution			Engage all relevant stakeholders and ensure requirements sign off
			Project manager ensure adequate change management
			Ensure adequate user acceptance testing
Poor vendor support			Ensure time zone constraints are allowed for via service level agreement
Impact of related projects			Active communications with IT project team
Lack of IT support staff (due to time constraints)			Active communications with IT project team

The table (sanitised) is a mix of actual examples from various clients.

Column 1 describes the risk and column 4 details what can be done to avoid it becoming an issue. Columns 2 and 3 are used to rate the severity of the risk threat.

To mitigate these risks, change managers are engaged. Therefore by extension, change managers are risk managers.

Now compare the table to the following typical position description for a change manager:

This position reports to the xx manager or executive and will be instrumental in providing change management expertise in support of organisation-wide business transformation, process reengineering and resulting system developments. The primary focus will be creating and implementing change management plans to maximise employee engagement and proactively manage employee and client resistance. The change management specialist will act as a coach for senior leaders and executives in helping them fulfil the role of change sponsor and will support project teams in integrating change management activities into their project plans. The role will involve liaising at all levels across business units to analyse and effectively develop, deliver and embed change management solutions in line with commercial objectives.

Quite clearly, there are overlaps between the risk mitigation actions and the change management position description. This raises the following fundamental question:

Why do change managers not formally link their change management plans to the risk register?

By way of example, the following is a change management plan I chose at random from a Google search:

Change Management Plan Template

Note: delete the prompts under each heading before submitting your plan.

Introduction
Provide background, link to strategic goals and other changes

Project Sponsor
This person leads the change project and is accountable for ensuring the project and change plan are implemented

Project Objectives
Detail what the project will achieve.

Change Objectives and Principles
Provide details of:
- What the change process will achieve [eg information sharing, engagement, input into system changes];
- Principles that underpin the change plan [eg inclusiveness/consultation, timeliness]; and
- Ethical issues that need to be considered and how will the change plan will address them.

Change Plan Elements
What are the main elements in the change plan? [eg people/culture, systems/technology, documentation, positions/roles, process, skills] Each of these elements may require a particular focus in the change plan.

Rationale for the Change
List the drivers and constraints for change.
What are the risks for the change process?

Key Stakeholder Analysis
Identify the key stakeholders [consider staff, other work units in SCU, management, unions, students and other clients] and:
- Analyse their response to the change [eg what will be their main concerns/fear, where is there likely to be support for the change];
- Identify their needs in terms of change management and consider the style of communication required [language style & level]; and
- Identify the preferred media for communicating or consulting with them about the change [eg sessions involving dialogue about the changes, newsletters, briefings from project team members, frequently asked questions].

Assessment of Readiness to Change
Comment on the status of the change so far [eg is there a high level strategy in place that stakeholders are already aware of and committed to that provides a framework for the change].
What elements might support the change [eg dissatisfaction with current processes; a workplace culture that supports change and innovation].
Is there strong senior support for the change?

Key Change Messages
Identify about 6 key messages to convey about the change process, being upfront about gains and losses. Consider:
- What will be gained/lost for the key stakeholder groups in the change process;
- The messages from the stakeholder perspective;
- What will be their main concerns; and
- Presenting changes in a positive light even whilst acknowledging loss.

Identify Change Elements
Structures/Processes/Responsiblities/Resources/Timeframes/Performance Measures
Consider the need for particular change support structures [eg a change team, super users/specialists who are trained first and can support people in the workplace, involvement of users/key stakeholders at various stages, change champions in the workplace].
Consider if there is a need for transitional arrangements to support and whether the introduction of the change process needs to be staged.
What will be the impact on workloads and how will these be managed?

Develop Change Plan
Develop a change plan including performance measures [how will you know the change plan is effective?]. Ensure the plan is adequately resourced.

From Southern Cross University at http://tiny.cc/n4nj1w.

This is a typical example of a change management plan. At a concept level I immediately question why a change management plan needs to exist as a separate document from the PID. However, if it is to be a stand-alone document, then there is no heading I would delete.

At no stage in completing the template is the author expected to link the change management plan to project risks. In fact, the word "risk" appears only once in the template, where the author is expected to describe risks to the change management process.

Based on this template, how can the project sponsor build confidence that project risks are being mitigated or that the change management activities will have any relevance to the risks at all?

My observation is that a risk register is typically prepared at the start of a project and then is really only given lip service throughout the course of the project. If the project manager does happen to review the register, then it's likely that the participants in the review meeting will readily explain how the risks are being managed and all is good. No panic required.

Equally and by contrast, my view is that change managers frequently start a project with a comparatively light definition of their project activities. Often with no more detail than the position description referred to above, supplemented with some reference to change activities such as weekly communications broadcasts, training plans, status reports, town hall meetings etc. Most likely they will have copied and pasted the relevant parts of the PID into the change management plan, if one exists at all. Then when the project begins they generally make it up as they go, using best and last experience as a guide.

My recommendation is that change management plans are retired as a separate document, replaced by the PID or SOW and that the role of the risk register is redefined so that it becomes a change management plan.

Risk Description	Likelihood	Impact	Mitigation Strategy	Change Management Methodology	Deliverables and Measures
Misaligned goals and objectives			Prepare the project definition document. Agree PID with stakeholders	Individual interviews with key stakeholders. Collective workshop to establish a common understanding of the goals and constraints of the project.	Common understanding of, and agreement on, goals and objectives of project. PID is endorsed and signed by all stakeholders.
Resistance to change			Administer an enlistment program.	Prepare a key stakeholder communications matrix. Individual interviews with key stakeholders to understand business drivers and constraints. Establish a calendar of regular meetings to update stakeholders on project status and to discuss concerns arising. Prepare a charter of support for project.	Key stakeholders have signed a charter of support for the project. Individual and collective agreement to support a request to change behaviour as required by the new business processes.
Insufficient budget			Prepare and socialise a detailed project definition document. Use document to prepare project budget. Apply a 20% risk loading.	Call a preliminary meeting with the steering committee to review project. Lead critical discussion on budget.	Budget agrees and aligned to scope, timeline and effort.
Insufficient resource allocation			Prepare and socialise a detailed project definition document. Confirm allocation of resources.	Extend the meeting with Steercom (above) to address resource allocation.	Resources aligned to scope, timeline and effort and committed to project.
Expectation to eliminate duplicate records not realised.			Engage all relevant stakeholders and ensure requirements sign off. Engage sites and branches around process.	Workshop with process owners to agree the "new mode of operation" that will deliver the anticipated savings. Train supervisors and staff in new mode of operation. Install KPIs and SLAs to support and monitor the behaviour and highlight areas of improvement. Establish correction action forum to review and address operational issues preventing the realisation of the project benefits. Eg Data issues.	For the new mode of operation: • Business process maps • Procedures • KPIs • SLAs • Trained staff • A corrective action forum.
Key stakeholders outside shared services reject solution			Engage all relevant stakeholders and ensure requirements sign off. Project manager ensure adequate change management. Ensure adequate user acceptance testing.	Prepare a key stakeholder communications matrix. Individual interviews with key stakeholders to understand business drivers and constraints. Establish a calendar of regular meetings to update stakeholders on project status and to discuss concerns arising. Prepare a charter of support for project.	Key stakeholders have signed a charter of support for the project.
Impact of related IT projects			Active communications with IT project team.	Include IT in Steercom. Establish a calendar of meetings with IT to discuss impact to "other" IT projects on current project.	IT is represented at Steercom. Calendar of meetings in place with IT.
Lack of IT support staff (due to time constraints)			Active communications with IT project team.	Include IT in Steercom. Establish a calendar of meetings with IT to review upcoming IT project resource requirements. Establish a resource requirements register with a 4 week forward view. Use weekly status reports to manage stakeholder expectations when project delays are to be expected due to resource or other constraints.	IT is represented at Steercom. Calendar of meetings in place with IT. Resource requirements register is in use.

This will ensure that:

1. Risk mitigation strategies are better thought through.
2. Change management is better aligned to the project.
3. Change managers understand their responsibilities more clearly.
4. Risks are continuously and actively managed, and
5. Project managers will have a structured means of evaluating the effectiveness of the change management aspect of the project.

Getting The Measure Of KPIs

I was talking to a client about Key Performance Indicators or KPIs and they passed me a large bound booklet. It must have had 200 pages. The booklet was their operations report; a compendium of KPIs. I was asked if I could assist to determine new KPIs to address performance issues within the business. I flicked through the booklet. It was filled with red and green status indicators. Mostly red. I handed the booklet back to the client and apologised—I could not help him. I pointed out that the book already held more KPIs than I could possibly think of, and that the problem was not the absence of a specific KPI, but rather the absence of response to the existing KPIs.

To elaborate this point, I turned to a page at random. The three-month trend report showed three months of red status indicators. This was largely the same for all the indicators on the page. The KPIs had been indicating an out of tolerance position for months and nothing had been done about it.

The conversation then moved to discussing the purpose of KPIs and how to make them effective in the business.

Frequently, when first implementing KPIs, the mindset is to measure everything that moves; if it doesn't move, kick it until it does and then measure it. Unfortunately, within a couple of months, many KPIs will be found to offer so little value that they are ignored. This sends a message to managers—that it's all talk and no action—and the slide to indifference starts.

There is only one reason to implement KPIs and that is to manage behaviour. Equally there is only one type of behaviour in an organisation and that is human behaviour. Companies don't behave, technology does not behave, plants and equipment do not behave. People behave. But what do KPIs measure? They measure customer satisfaction, mileage on trucks, lost sales, revenues, costs, throughput, quality and productivity. The list is endless.

The underlying principle of a KPI is—if you are going to manage it, then measure it, otherwise ignore it. There is no point in measuring something you are not going to manage. To address an indicator that is out of tolerance, somebody somewhere in the organisation has to do something differently. Different to what they did last time because last time they created an out of tolerance result.

The difficulty arises when the KPIs are too broad in their definition. For example, sales are down so salespeople are told to "get out there" and work harder. But does the salesperson know what to do differently to improve their sales figures? Clearly their current approach is not working. They need to ask themselves, "What must I do differently to ensure I get a different result?" Or in other words, "How must I change my behaviour?"

The astute sales manager will know exactly what behaviours are required to make even an inept salesperson successful and they will implement KPIs that evaluate this behaviour at the micro level. The focus will be on things that the manager can actually change. This could be number of calls made, length of calls, number of times the salesperson gets through to the decision-maker, appointments set and the number of times a salesperson's telephone rings.

The misconception is that sales managers are in sales, or more broadly, that managers of a function are in that function. The truth is they are not. They are in a separate function called management and managers behave differently to workers (staff). Therefore the KPIs that measure a manager's behaviour must be different to those that measure staff behaviour—even if they appear to be in the same function.

The seniority between managers introduces additional complexities.

Consider the following four relationships.

The first relationship is between first-line management and staff. A key feature of this relationship is that the two roles are different. Broadly, staff members deliver technical output while managers deliver an administrative output. This requires that the manager use KPIs that measure *technical* behaviour.

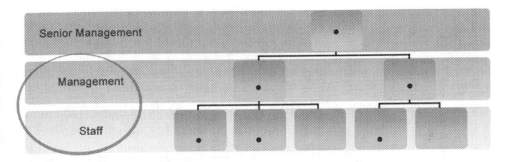

The second relationship is between a manager who manages workers and his/her manager.

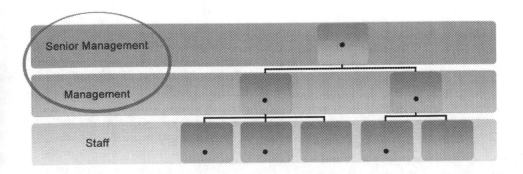

The next level is the relationship between two levels of management where neither level manages worker.

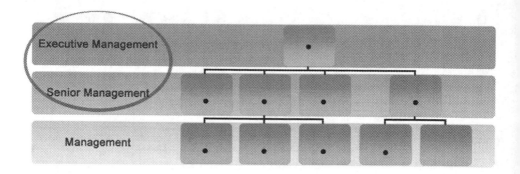

The key feature of the previous two levels is that management is managing management. This requires the use of KPIs that measure *management behaviour*. The KPIs for each level can largely be the same, separated by the degree of aggregation applied to the more senior of the roles.

The fourth level is the relationship between directors and managers. In many respects this relationship is similar to the first level of management. From a director's point of view, business management is *"technical delivery"* whilst directors take more of a deterministic/directive role in the organisation in that they determine strategy, the governance model, the organisational risk appetite etc.

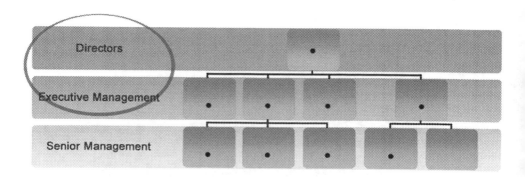

For each relationship set, what is the role of the senior manager? This is a complex question and not easily answered in a short paragraph. But in the spirit of this article I will say it is to ensure that direct reports are *behaving in a manner that maximises the likelihood of them achieving their KPIs.*

Based on this definition, for each relationship, it is mandatory that the senior of the two managers knows what behaviour is required to maximise the business benefit possible from the subordinate management function, and what behavioural changes are required when the expected business benefit is not realised.

If the relationship between the KPI and behaviour is not understood, or if a KPI cannot be manipulated through changes in a manager's behaviour, then it is likely that the wrong KPI is being used.

Malicious Compliance:
The Smiling Serpent

I was talking to a colleague last week over a beer. He was extremely disgruntled as he related the story of his day. Basically it went like this:

I have been working on this IT project for months, doing long days and occasional weekends. This morning I arrived at 10:15 a.m. In front of everyone the project manager shouted at me that the project hours were 8:45 a.m. to 5 p.m. and that I should make sure my timesheet reflected my late start. Not only was I embarrassed by the reprimand, but the project manager gave me no credit for the fact that I never left the project before 6 p.m.—ever.

I asked him what he was going to do about it. His answer was simple. "I will work the project hours, no more, no less," he said. "Then when the project is not delivered on time, it will be the PM's fault, not mine."

At the time of writing, he has been true to his word and is working what he calls short days.

I reflected on his story and I recognised that at some point in our professional lives, we have all stood in front of a manager, receiving a dressing-down. Outwardly we maintained our professional demeanour, while inwardly we were seething. The situation for which we were reprimanded may have been our fault, but our motives were honourable. We were working in the best interests of the project and of our colleagues. In our mind the reprimand was just wrong.

After such a reprimand it is quite human to leave the manager's office with a mind-set of, "Stick it buddy, if you don't want me to do 'x,' then I won't. It's by the book from here on in."

For most of us the emotion subsides fairly quickly and we get on with our job, recognising that we can't please all of the people, all of the time.

The problem is that there is a minority group who do not forgive and forget quite so easily. For these people, their chagrin runs deep and they cannot readily bounce back from a reprimand. These people take their "by the book" vow to heart and they consciously set out to change their behaviour for the worse. Next time the manager asks them to do something they follow the instruction to the letter, entirely aware that what they were asked to do is not what the manager actually wants. They know full well that following the instruction to the letter will be counterproductive to the manager's intent and for that reason alone, they do exactly that.

This dogmatic adherence to the exact instruction given, rather than to the intent of the instruction is termed malicious compliance.

From a business or project point of view, malicious compliance is a treacherous form of corporate sabotage. It can be very difficult to identify and even more difficult to treat. It can manifest in many ways including adhering strongly to shift start and stop times, not contributing to a discussion when you know the answer unless you are asked a direct question, exaggerated responses to instructions, working strictly to the agreed standard or preparing reports you know to be unnecessary or irrelevant.

Failure to identify malicious compliance can set a project back months or, as I have seen in some cases, derail the project altogether. This is especially true if the bad apple is a leader in the group. For example, if the leader starts to work to the standard hours then it won't be long before the whole group is following suit. Equally if the leader's attitude goes unchecked, it won't be long before the whole group is grumbling and questioning the authority and leadership of the (project) manager. This can force an unplanned change of management as that becomes the only option to bring the situation back to normal. This in turn could unfortunately reinforce the negative behaviour of the employee or group and it may be some time before management is able to get the balance of power back.

The trigger for resorting to malicious compliance will vary by individual and includes everything from an individual's need to implement a Machiavellian private political agenda of destabilisation, to those who are suffering change fatigue and need to resort to doing the minimum just to get by.

I consider those who are Machiavellian to be smiling serpents. They smile to your face while sabotaging your project. They have perfected the art of hiding in the open.

For an employee to be maliciously compliant requires the employee's manager to know that the employee could do a better job if they wanted to. It is a case of "can but won't" as opposed to "can't and won't." The difference between the two is motivation. The former's motivation will always be negative and the latter's could be neutral or positive.

Most people cannot maintain the rage for long and generally do not require remedial action beyond possibly having a chat with them after the emotion has passed. For this majority, bouts of malicious compliance should be seen as part of the process of building corporate experience and maturing as a professional. For them, it is a matter of learning that you can get angry and then get over it.

For the few that do persevere with malicious compliance there are three remedies:

1.   Discuss outcomes and show belief in the person.
2.   Give short instructions.
3.   Listen to them, they might be right.

Moving the discussion to outcomes forces the staff member to answer the question of "so what?"

"You fulfilled the instruction—so what? What did you achieve?"

Forcing the employee to confront their contribution, or lack thereof, is a powerful means of communicating that malicious compliance cannot produce satisfactory results and that obvious and continued mediocrity cannot be ignored by either party. Both need to take action.

By definition, malicious compliance is a conscious choice. The employee chooses to behave in this manner. Therefore, they can choose to relax their stance as well. In the first remedy listed above, I mention that the manager should show belief in the person. This is especially important when the employee cannot see a way out of the situation they have created. By accepting their justifications at face value and showing belief in them as a person, the manager allows the person to save face. This gives the person room to move, to adjust their behaviour without having to fully admit fault. It should lead to the return of an acceptable level of output and behaviour.

As part of addressing the issue, the manager should give the employee short and simple instructions where the deliverable is easily identifiable and within a short timeframe. This allows the employee to build success upon success and to receive positive feedback frequently. It will help to mitigate any self-esteem issues the person may have.

Equally, these two remedies will provide the manager with the sufficient case study material should it become necessary to begin a job transfer or termination procedure. Because—if you can't change the people, then change the people.

The third remedy is to critically listen to the employee. If the employee is a person with obvious skills and talent who is in effect dumbing themselves down to conform to the instructions, the manager must evaluate exactly who the dogmatic party is. This is particularly true when a manager is dealing with a highly experienced technical person. In this case the manager may not fully understand the technical answers given to their questions and therefore they inappropriately instruct the technician into a course of action the technician knows to be wrong. The technician is unable to get the manager to understand the error in the instruction so they throw up their hands and say, "It's not my problem, I will do what I am told."

It's Only Kinky The First Time

Everybody on this planet knows that cutlery goes in the top drawer. You can walk into any kitchen anywhere and know that if you need cutlery, then one of the top drawers will have it. But not in my house. My wife looked at the dust and crumbs etc. that kept falling off the counter into the cutlery drawer and watched the family behaviour. She noticed that a person would open the drawer, take out an item and frequently not fully close the drawer. This meant that anything falling off the counter got caught in the drawer.

Her solution was to move the cutlery to the second drawer down so it could be closed with the upper leg or hip. The action would be unconscious. Your mind is focussed on what is happening on the counter and with unconscious multitasking you also close the drawer. If for no other reason than an open drawer is in the way.

The solution works brilliantly. The drawer is substantially cleaner. The problem is that I have over 40 years of training behind me that says cutlery goes in the top drawer. It took me a week to accept that cutlery could live in the second drawer. I also realise that despite all my consulting and experience in change management I was resistant to change. My wife implemented the change, not through consultation and facilitated workshops but through active execution of strategy. On my part, while I was not happy for a few days, I soon realised that the roof of my house had not fallen down and the quality of my days did not diminish. If anything my life span has probably been extended through having cleaner cutlery.

If you can't cope with change at home, how do you cope with it at work? A quick scan of the job boards indicates multiple vacancies for change managers with job descriptions that variously include everything from process mapping and training to communications and stakeholder management depending on the definition being used. This got me thinking.

What needs to change for things to be different in an organisation?

I now take my cutlery out of the second drawer at home, but I remain convinced that if I ever find myself living on my own, my cutlery will be in the top drawer.

So my behaviour has changed but my mind hasn't. My "boss" told me to do things differently so I did. But given that I am never the one to actually clean the cutlery drawer I have not actively enjoyed the benefit.

To truly effect change in a business it is mandatory to engage the hearts and minds of the "changees." Training staff to use a tool such as a newly implemented ERP solution gives them new skills, but that does not make them embrace change.

Popular literature often refers to the WIIFM—"what's in it for me." This is an important question. People change for two reasons. 1. The pain of maintaining the status quo is too high and 2. the pleasure foregone by not changing is too irresistible to forego. Any other point in this spectrum is unlikely to cause a person to want to change. The key word is "want." They may have to change to keep their job, but that does not mean they want to. For change to be sustainable, people have to want to change. The old joke—*How many consultants does it take to change a light bulb? Just one, but the light bulb has to want to change."*– is particularly relevant.

For most projects the pain and pleasure points are understood by the project sponsor and the senior managers. They have commissioned the project and understand the ROI. In the majority of cases, these managers are not directly impacted by the project. They receive the benefits but do not actively work in the business functions and processes that produce the benefits. Obviously it is not black and white, but in broad terms they consume benefit and do not generate benefit. For these managers it is very easy to embrace change. Quite possibly they don't even have to change their behaviour at all.

For the employees who work in the business, it is a completely different story. They have to change and change means learning a brand new routine — learning a brand new set of habits. But the benefit of change to these staff is diluted. They sit towards the middle of the pleasure/pain spectrum and are unlikely to receive any tangible benefit from change — so why bother changing? This brings us to the WIIFM question. An answer frequently heard is that you get to keep your job. Sure this is a nice outcome, but it is not one that is going to capture the hearts and minds of the staff.

To capture the hearts and minds you need to enlist the staff. Enlisting staff means creating an environment where they are willing to proactively break their comfort zone, to challenge their entrenched views and truly believe that things will be better as a result of the change. This may mean pushing them kicking and screaming over the edge so they realise that change was safe. Show them that it is only kinky the first time. The next time it is familiar – *I have done it before and survived.* Once you have done something once, you are more willing to do it again.

How do you enlist staff? The most important thing is to realise there is no such thing as "staff" in the sense that "staff" is a collective noun. There are people, individuals. Each person is different, with different agendas, hopes and fears and personal pressures. To treat them as a collective is to shortcut the enlistment process. There really is no substitute for open communication, consultation and active engagement of the individuals.

I readily accept that it is frequently impossible to engage each person in a one-on-one environment. This does not defeat the point. Rather treat one-on-one as the benchmark and the process of getting there as a process of continuous improvement. Where you have a choice, err on the side of engaging with small groups.

I also readily accept that there will always be individuals who will not accept change under any circumstances. In this case, acknowledge it, move on and let the normal course of events for employee lifecycle management play out. As my mentor used to say—if you can't change the people, change the people.

Show Me The Money

Recently I spent a morning with a colleague discussing ideas for a new business. He is working on a number of excellent business models and if he can commercialise them, he should do very well.

He asked if I could assist him to "clear his head." He was too close to the detail and the ideas and concepts were beginning to blur.

My immediate suggestions were:
1. Draw the business.
2. Follow the money.

We spent the next two hours on exactly these two points. What he initially thought was a simple question, and one that he already had straight in his head, proved to be quite complex. It is amazing how a person can jump large chasms in a single bound in his/her head.

Our conversation produced a new and annotated picture of the proposed business depicting how it would work and the flow of money. It was completely different to the picture he initially had in his head and it substantially changed the business case and intended architecture. Importantly it resolved a number of the mental blocks he had about the business. The blocks existed as subconsciously he knew there were issues; he just could not articulate where. Following the money is a sure way of resolving this problem.

This same difficulty constantly plays out on a large scale with my clients. As a consultant, I am frequently engaged to prepare process models, maps and related material. The conversation generally revolves around the relationship between people, process and technology and is often interlaced with the phrase "shared service."

What I battle to understand is this: why, despite engaging consultants to investigate the business, are managers so reluctant to engage with the detail? Businesses are complex, but managers just don't seem to want to know.

To further illustrate this point, the next graphic is an example of a detailed process map. Call it "Process 1." I do not expect managers to invest significant time at this level of detail. That is, managers other than the process owner.

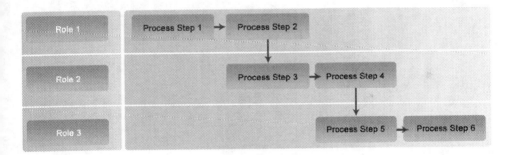

Occasionally, an individual process map will include a reference to the next process in the sequence. More often than not, the process just ends with a box that says "post invoice" or "file letter" or "pay supplier." That's it. Process over.

This style of process mapping has little bearing on reality. Activity very seldom just stops in a business. Rather there is a handover to the next department or process. Everybody knows this and automatically accepts that this detail is just not included on individual process maps.

But, when that process map is placed in conjunction with other processes on the value chain, it offers limited insight. When the same process is shown inclusive of its relationships to other processes the value of the analysis goes up significantly. Consider the two graphics on the next page.

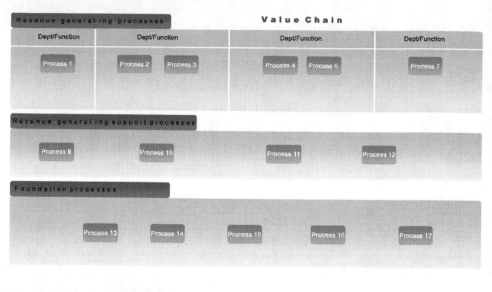

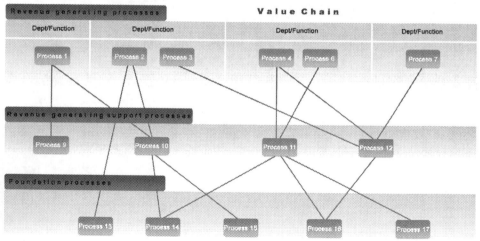

The top graphic shows what processes sit where on the framework. The graphic below shows the relationships between them. The interconnecting lines represent the hand off between processes and the flow of information within the business.

The top row of each graphic represents the functions and processes that generate revenue. This row answers the question, "How do I make money?" The middle row comprises the processes that support revenue generation. These processes are not customer facing and exist only because revenue is flowing. The bottom row comprises the processes that must exist for the company to be in business, in other words, the true back office.

Rows 2 and 3 tend to be the areas where you spend money. In rough terms row 2 goes to gross contribution and row 3 to operating expenses.

The layout is a great way to "show me the money." It tells you which processes result in revenue and how and where the invoice is generated. It also provides a foundation for determining which processes belong in the shared services group and the basic configuration of that group. By extension it supports the demarcation of service level agreements and key performance indicators.

A simple critique of the graphic demonstrates that there is possibly a significant gap in the revenue flow.

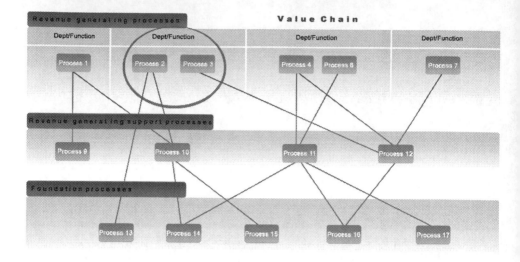

Within the circle there is no output process for the third process. It is a revenue generating process but it is almost 100% independent of all other processes. This can't be right. Equally getting to its trigger process seems somewhat convoluted.

This insight is enormously valuable, especially if a company wants to implement or refine a shared services model.

If this reasonably simple diagram produces this type of value, why then are managers reluctant to engage in the detail? Without the detail the above issue would not be exposed. Yet it can easily be consulting suicide to put the graphic up for comment. There is a good chance you will hear, "It's too complex, and I can't understand it." So you "dumb it down" to a point where it fits on a slide and uses large font.

I fully acknowledge there is a time and a place for getting into the detail and presentations should be tailored to the audience.

I close with the comment that businesses are complex places and managers should make the effort and take the time to understand them. At the very minimum they should understand the flow of money. Where is it generated? Where and when it is invoiced? And how is it spent? Not necessarily at the fine detail level, but most certainly at the building block level.

Perception:
It's Not What You Think

"Maybe each human being lives in a unique world, a private world different from those inhabited and experienced by all other humans . . . If reality differs from person to person, can we speak of reality singular, or shouldn't we really be talking about plural realities? And if there are plural realities, are some more true (more real) than others? What about the world of a schizophrenic? Maybe it's as real as our world. Maybe we cannot say that we are in touch with reality and he is not, but should instead say, his reality is so different from ours that he can't explain his to us, and we can't explain ours to him. The problem, then, is that if subjective worlds are experienced too differently, there occurs a breakdown in communication . . . and there is the real illness."

I read the above quote by Philip K. Dick and it reinforced how relevant perception is to change management and the importance of what we say and allow others to say.

This was first highlighted to me when I was working with IBM on the Mercedes-Benz South Africa business transformation project. In the early part of the project we spent considerable time collecting data, the bulk of which was qualitative. I asked the seasoned project manager on what basis we could rely on qualitative data to make far-reaching recommendations. His reply was: if enough people repeat something to be true, then it is true, irrespective of the facts. In other words, perception is reality.

The primary agenda of any change management program is to deliver a change in behaviour. This is equally true for very large programs such as national "Don't Drink and Drive" campaigns to small localised programs, internal to a business, such as how to code an invoice properly. In all cases people only change when they perceive the need to change, and it is the change manager's role to socialise a message that will create this perception at the individual level and within the crowd.

It is not difficult to determine the view of the crowd as people will readily repeat what they perceive to be a commonly held truth. It is considerably more difficult to reliably determine how an individual perceives the world as their views are coloured by an unlimited range of personal circumstances to which the change manager is not privy. Consequently, it is a waste of time to try and change an individual's foundation perceptions.

Rather the change manager should focus on managing how individuals express their perception of the work environment and the changes within it.

The importance of managing perception is represented by the dip in the graphic.

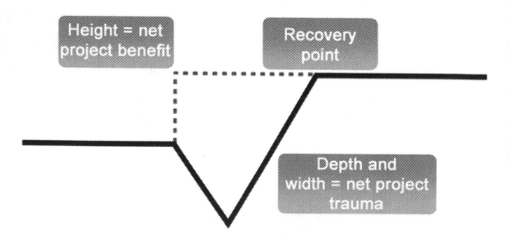

Every business transformation project shakes up the organisation. People become uncertain and routines are disrupted. This will cause organisational performance to decline, as represented by the dip, before targeted improvements are realised. As people become disrupted they lash out in their language.

Statements such as "nothing works here" or "management are idiots" or "why bother, nobody cares" become increasingly common and indicate a low level of engagement. The less engaged a person is, the more they will resort to using sweeping statements instead of taking the time to consider what is truly bothering them before they speak. These types of statement only serve to widen and deepen the gap and make the change program appear more confronting than it actually is.

Without intervention, and without a message to the opposite, there is a real danger that the sweeping statements of an individual become the view of the crowd. *It must be true if everybody is saying it.* Consider a new hire stepping into that environment. What else could they realistically believe?

The change manager cannot change how a person feels. However, the change manager can change the way people express themselves.

Instead of condoning or ignoring sweeping statements such as "this software is useless" ask staff to be specific with their complaints. Persist until they come up with a specific concern like "I can't print a copy invoice." That is the real problem. Encouraging individuals to replace sweeping statements with specific statements will cause them to actively think about and engage with the issue. When people *speak* differently they allow themselves to *think* differently and they start to *perceive* the world differently. This tends to reduce emotion and exaggeration. In addition, when people know that they will be called out on a broad generalisation, they tend to become more circumspect in what they say. Eventually they may even behave differently.

From a change management point of view, it is far better for staff to know that they cannot print a copy invoice than to believe the software is completely useless. Then, when they are complaining to other staff, they will be accurate and specific, not vague and inaccurate. The crowd becomes infected with the truth, which is, in this case, that you can't print a copy invoice, rather than by broad inaccuracies about perceived deficiencies in the software.

Only when a person changes the way they express themselves, will they really be able to change the way they perceive their work environment, and subsequently change the way they present themselves in the work environment. Occasionally you will hear that someone has had a real change of attitude. What this really means is that their language has changed, from negative to positive. When people say positive things their colleagues will respond positively.

The same can apply to the group, but to achieve it the change manager needs to introduce a common vocabulary, a company lexicon. It will promote an environment where individuals use the same words for the same things. That way everybody knows what is meant when statements are made. Conversations should get shorter and the disquiet caused by miscommunication should be reduced. Introducing a common vocabulary is exceptionally difficult. It requires that the change manager has the vocabulary to start with and a mind-set that realises that change management is not just about training people in a technical skill.

I recognise, that despite the change manager's best efforts, it is impossible to get everyone in an entire organisation to change the way they speak. The best mitigation is to introduce scorecards. Using a scorecard moves the conversation from subjective perceptions about what happened to factual data. It should cause the conversation to start with a discussion on actual business results rather than a particular person's behaviour, or more importantly, the manager's perception of the employee's behaviour.

I close with the thought that trying to manage perception is similar to standing in a hall between two mirrors. Each mirror reflects the other and this continues until each mirror appears to have an infinite number of reflections in it. These reflections represent the perceptions two people could have of each other. To know which two "perceptions" are active in the conversation is impossible.

Managing Change

Background

My views on change management were forged by the 14 months I spent on the Mercedes Benz South Africa (MBSA) project. The project ran for a few years commencing in 1995.

The date is relevant, as the country had just started taking its first steps as a full democracy. The memory of the apartheid years was fresh in the minds of all, especially in those of the local labour force, most of whom had borne the brunt of some of the worst aspects of the apartheid regime.

The project was a large transformation project affecting most areas of the business. Success could only be achieved if the workforce supported the transformation and based on the country's recent history, this level of trust would be very difficult to achieve.

An important point to note: this article in no way implies that MBSA supported or endorsed the apartheid regime. Rather, the difficulties I refer to were experienced by the workers on a daily basis just by living in the country.

The MBSA Project

A project team was assembled with experts flying in from all over the world. MBSA allocated approximately 70 full-time staff to the project.

We kicked off the project with a three-day off-site conference. The agenda was to make sure that everyone on the team understood the vision, the methodology and the toolsets we would be using. (There was also time for team-building, normally over a bottle of Meerlust Rubicon '77, a particularly fine wine.)

The project followed the normal course of any large transformation. Data collection, analysis, visioning etc. Interlaced throughout this activity was a change management program.

The program employed a number of communication techniques including everything from posters and brochures, to live theatre and town hall meetings.

The posters and brochures were professionally produced, multilingual and widely distributed. The theatre was delivered by professional actors. The themes were designed to mimic how MBSA treated their customers and the consequential customer reaction. It was very confronting. This theatre was played out in all locations all over the country. It told the story of why change was necessary.

The town hall meetings were carefully managed affairs often held at an outside venue. The conference rooms were transformed with MBSA branding—and when you stepped into the room, you knew you were somewhere special. The meetings were also held all over the country, so every location felt included. This meant that MBSA often had the entire transformation team and scores of staff and management driving or flying hundreds of kilometres. The cost would have been enormous. Typically an event would have 500 people in attendance.

At each session the Managing Director would make a presentation acknowledging issues and/or describing the future. The trade unions were invited to these sessions and were privy to all the presentations.

The intent of the communications package was to ensure that everyone in the organisation was aware of the need for change, what could be expected from the project and how they could communicate their concerns back to management.

For me, the crowning moment of the change management program was when the trade union members stood up—unannounced—at a town hall meeting, and started singing songs of support for the program. What was once an adversarial relationship was quickly becoming a relationship based on respect and a common desire to address the issues in the company. It was a highly emotional moment and instantly became my benchmark for what a well-orchestrated change management program could achieve.

In summary the characteristics of the MBSA change management program were:

1. A well-funded, well-staffed, cohesive project team.
2. A well-funded, dedicated change program.
3. A broad selection of communication techniques catering for all levels of literacy and learning preferences.
4. A substantial allocation of time to the change program.
5. Strong participation and leadership from the Managing Director down.
6. Management went to the people. (Staff was not called to a head office presentation.)
7. Honesty.
8. Willingness to actively listen and respond to feedback.

What we can learn

In the time since the Mercedes Benz South Africa project, I have not seen another like it. The major difference between MBSA and subsequent projects I have witnessed is the restriction on time and money. Project leaders almost always acknowledge the need for a dedicated change management program but frequently this desire does not translate into sufficient funds, time or active engagement from the leadership. Mostly a business will hire a change manager and consider the change management job done. But just because you have a change manager does not mean you have a change program.

Two dimensions to change management

There are two dimensions to change management.

The first dimension is the organisational level view. The second is recognition of each individual in the business.

The first engages the hearts and minds of all stakeholders. The focus is on establishing a common and pervasive understanding of the need for change, and then ensuring that each person is aware of their responsibilities in assisting change to happen.

The second is actually changing the behaviour of the individual. Even with a comprehensive change management program, it does not mean that an individual will actually decide to modify their behaviour.

Effective change management at the organisational level requires that the business give it a formal mandate. This means that its importance is recognised and that it has a formal structure.

An effective change management structure typically has four levels:

1. The steering committee
2. The working committee
3. The project teams
4. The program office

The **steering committee** sets the project strategy and ensures the projects are delivering change in line with the strategic intent of the company.

The **working committee** is the primary engine for driving change in the business. Its purpose is to establish and manage the project teams that will gather and synthesise data and then to discuss this data and make recommendations to the steering committee.

The **project teams** are task-focused groups, typically made up of staff members who have been seconded full-time to the project, part-time subject matter experts and business consultants who may provide methodology and other specialist skills.

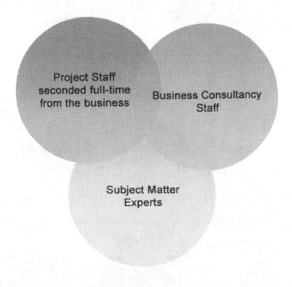

The **program office** ensures this change hierarchy is managed for success. It provides the tools and resources, and allocates the budget to ensure the desired outcomes can be achieved. It should restrict its role to librarian and scorekeeper. It is not on the field of play, but watching the play. This ensures that it does not inadvertently impede the business from taking ownership of change. It is important to note that the business *provides* the budget. The program office *allocates* the budget.

Putting it all together you get:

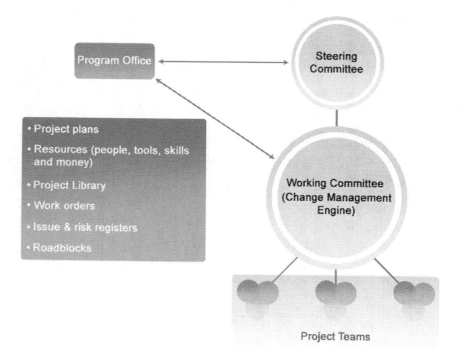

The project teams can either be orientated by function or service line, i.e., a finance team that examines everything in finance, or a process team that examines all processes in the business. In the former, the subject matter expert is the process person and in the latter the subject matter expert is the finance representative.

I consider it essential that one of the project teams is a communications team, with the sole focus of communicating the "project" to the business and ensuring that the business can communicate with the project.

Bringing "business as usual" into the picture you get:

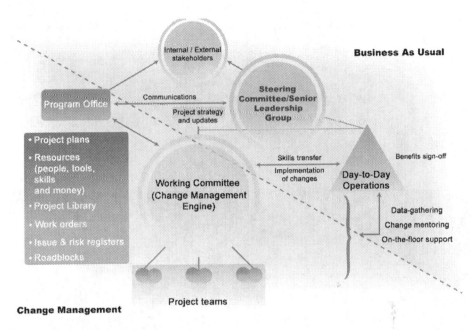

Those who are charged with leading *business as usual* get on with running the business, and the project teams engage with the business to better understand the issues and discuss improvements.

If the business is willing to fully formalise this approach then the above structure will include a corrective action team (CAT) as a second essential project team. The various project teams can come and go as required, but the CAT and the communications team become permanent fixtures.

Many project leaders I speak to consider their projects to be too small for such a formal communications management role. To mitigate this constraint, the communications process should still be formalised, but the staffing becomes part-time.

I learnt a long time ago the formula for rumour. It is rumour = ambiguity x interest.

With a project there is always interest. Good communications will dilute the ambiguity.

There are two aspects to preparing a structured communications package. These are the message itself and the management of the message. Each has sub attributes.

Message	Management
Content	Collect
Relevance	Store
Accuracy	Process
Timeliness	Distribute
Access	
Support	

Source: Russell Swanborough

For the message, consider:

- Who is going to read the content and why is it relevant to them?
- What is the level of accuracy required?
- Will broad brush statements suffice or is it important to include numbers to the second decimal point?

- When is the information needed and how will it be accessed?
- If there are questions, who do they turn to for support?

The answers to these questions will determine the physical attributes of the message.

For example, a senior executive is accustomed to working with electronic messages anywhere in the world. A factory worker may want to be addressed personally in a town hall meeting, where they can evaluate first-hand the "trustworthiness" of the messenger. Management of the message includes answering the questions: Where does the raw data come from? How do I reply to it? Where/how can I access it at a later stage?

To briefly summarise the concept behind the corrective action team, the business gets on with day-to-day operations. When non-conformance to requirements is identified through normal business activity, then it is up to the management structure to address the issue. In the event that they are not able to permanently resolve the underlying issue that caused the non-conformance, then they will raise a CAR (corrective action request) and lodge it with the CAT. The CAT will work with the other project teams to fully diagnose the underlying issue and will recommend actions to the working committee to permanently resolve the problem. The working committee reviews and endorses the recommendations and the business is asked to implement the change and to monitor its effectiveness. The project teams should assist with implementation.

As this corrective action process gets better and stronger, a culture of continuous improvement emerges and the change management structure evolves and transforms from being a vehicle set up to deliver a project to become a vehicle that delivers excellence in the business.

This brings us to the **second dimension of change management—** changing the individual.

When a person is asked to change their routine and habits they generally go through three stages of change.

Suitable terms for these stages are:

1. Mechanistic
2. Conceptual
3. Adoption

Source: Proudfoot Plc

The **mechanistic** stage is the toughest. This is when an individual is most resistant to change. They are questioning the relevance of the change, and often say that while they fully support the change, it does not apply to their role. Often staff will attend meetings or training on the new approach and be positive in the session. Afterwards they return to their work area and tell their staff, "That's all rubbish, those folk in their fancy suits don't know what they are talking about and it will never work here. We will continue doing what we have always done."

To resolve this mind-set the change manager needs to work with the individual staff members and often the best approach is JFDI: "Just do it." The individual is forced to comply. They do not have to fully understand why the change is important; they only have to adopt the new way of doing things.

Over a period of time—which could be hours, days or weeks—the penny will drop, and the staff member will start to see the benefits of doing it the new way.

This is the second stage—**conceptual understanding**. At this point they will start to introduce positive improvements and customisations to make the changes more relevant and appropriate to their area.

As this happens they move to the third stage—**adoption.** They now have full ownership of the changes and consider them their own. Asking them to make further changes at this time becomes difficult as they will be back to stage 1.

To move a person through these three stages requires extensive "on-the-floor" support. The change agent needs to be working with the business on a daily basis to help implement the changes.

The expected level of resistance can be plotted in the following matrix:

	Can	Can't
Will	Encourage Role model Use as change leader	On-the-job training Mentor Celebrate achievement
Won't	Counsel Support On-the-job mentoring	Counsel Consider reallocation to other duties

Source: Generic model

The key is to identify those staff that **Can** work in the new way of doing things and who **Will** work with you and use them as change leaders/role models. These staff members require the least amount of effort.

Staff that **Will** work with you but lack the skills to do so (**Can't**) are the next easiest group. Their minds are open and they are willing to learn. Give them training and mentoring to embed the new routines. It is important not to underestimate the amount of time these people need to embed the change. Without on-going mentoring, the changes may become too difficult and the person may slip into the **Won't/Can't** category.

The third category is **Can/Won't**. This person has the skills to work in the new way but is resistant to doing so. They are firmly entrenched in stage 1. This person is most dangerous to the change program. Other staff will watch how this person is dealt with and may take their lead from him/her. This person requires extensive "on-the-floor" support and the JFDI approach should be strictly enforced. If you can switch this person from a **Can/Won't** to a **Can/Will**, then you may have the best change champion you could ask for.

The last category is **Can't/Won't**. This person needs counselling to help them understand their position and extensive "on-the-floor" support. If they do not show signs of moving to **Can/Won't** or **Will/Can't** then they are probably not suited to that role. The maxim is—if you can't change the people, change the people. Unfortunately this is sometimes required.

The typical progression between categories is shown below:

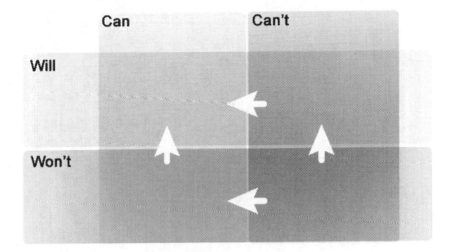

It can be said that the only time change is real is when it is at the level of the individual. Concepts such as "organisational change" or "business transformation" are valid phrases and have specific meaning. But they can also be misleading. Businesses don't actually exist. They are legal constructs. What exists are the elements of the business—the people/plant/machinery/money etc.

To change a business means that you need to change the relationships between the elements. "People" refers to the staff members and this means actual change takes place at the individual level.

In closing I come back to the two dimensions of a change program:

1. **Engage the hearts and minds of all stakeholders.** Use this dimension to address the **Will/Won't** aspect. Get the staff to a mind-set of **Will**.
2. **Change the behaviour of the individual.** Use this dimension to address the **Can/Can't** aspect.

The Risk of Risk Management

Last year I published an article on governance and a number of people wrote to me, critiquing the article over its failure to adequately include risk as a separate item in the frameworks I was using. Their point was that while risk management is an integral and mandatory discipline for executive management and company directors, it is sufficiently important for it to be addressed as an item in its own right.

I agree with this point of view but am not convinced that risk management is something separate from the day-to-day running of the business. To be fair I don't think the people critiquing my article intended that risk be separated from the business; rather their view was that it is a specific discipline and it requires special emphasis in the business. This is particularly true as the operational time horizon shifts from tactical to strategic for the more senior levels of management in the organisation. This includes directors.

At the senior levels, the strength of the focus on risk is so strong that risk is frequently governed through a stand-alone committee (risk or risk and audit committee) or through a specialised role such as chief/senior/global risk manager.

The problem is that best practice (of any sort) embraced at senior levels, frequently, does not filter down to the operational level. And when it comes to risk management this schism remains unchecked by the advisory community (consultants etc.) and tactical risk plans seldom, if ever, adequately reference the strategic risk frameworks that are used at the senior levels in the organisation.

The majority of the tactical risk management plans comprise the same elements: **Identify** and **Assess**, **Evaluate**, **Manage** and **Measure**.

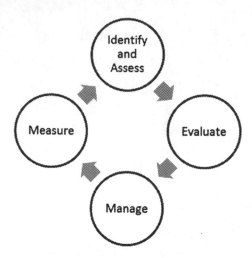

While the verbs may change from model to model and author to author, the intent remains consistent between the various models.

The standard approach at the tactical level is to hold workshops to identify and assess and evaluate the risks facing the business or project. Comprehensive lists of risks are produced.

My view is that these workshops fall foul of the principle that "you don't know what you don't know" and therefore it should be expected that important risks will be missed. This is the risk of risk management.

It is impossible to remove the problem of "you don't know what you don't know," but it is possible to mitigate it if you change where you start, and you don't start with **Identify**.

My recommendation is that the preparation of a tactical risk management plan should start with an articulation of company culture and a reaffirmation of the risk appetite of the business. Risk appetite can be defined as the nature and extent of risk a company is *willing* to take in order to meet its medium to long-term strategic objectives. To have clarity on risk appetite demands that the business understand exactly what business it is in and whether the business strategy is aligned to the business itself. For example, the major food retailers are not really in the business of selling food. Rather they are in the treasury business. Every day they collect millions in cash deposits and therefore have no problems with accounts receivable. On the other hand, they pay suppliers slowly. Their true business is to invest and grow the funds in between.

Confirming there is a common understanding of the company culture is important. The simple definition of culture is "the way we do things around here" and the risk appetite should be aligned to the culture. Obviously a high risk appetite will not fit a company with a highly conservative culture.

Risk appetite is different to risk tolerance in that risk tolerance defines how much of each risk type the business will accept. It is the risk parameter for each risk type. Risk tolerance allows the risk appetite to be broken down into measurable components.

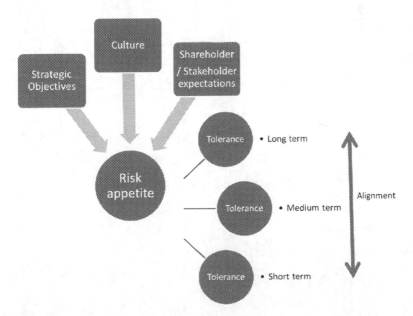

I am not suggesting that the team preparing a tactical risk management plan should start with redefining the culture in the company. Rather they should make sure that everyone agrees what the culture is and make sure they fully understand the risk appetite and associated tolerances for the business.

At the tactical level, the **Identify** activity then becomes an exercise in aligning identified tactical risks to the short-term tolerance levels. This will ensure the tactical risk management plan is aligned to types and areas of risk the company is willing to embrace as risk tolerance is informed by risk appetite. It also encourages the completeness of thought around tactical risks. A quick review for "widows and orphans," between the tolerances and the tactical risk plan, should quickly identify missed or non-aligned risks.

Using risk tolerance means that you already have the parameters for your risk model. This does not mean that the parameters at the tactical level mirror those of the strategic level, but there should be some obvious alignment.

From a risk management point of view you are now in a strong position to **Identify** and **Assess**, **Evaluate** and **Manage** risks.

The **Manage** step can be complex and the title is misleading. A more fitting title would be **Protect**, as in how does the company protect itself against risk? There are three primary defences:

1. Self-insure
2. Transfer risk—external insurance
3. Reduce risk—operational response

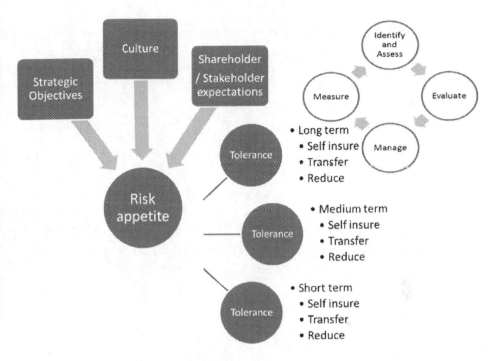

These three choices should be used concurrently. The weighting between each protection option is determined by the risk appetite, the specific risk under consideration and the time horizon associated with that risk.

By way of example, consider reputational risk. There is little point taking internal or external insurance against reputational risk as once it manifests you can't undo it. You can't un-sink a cruise liner or un-crash a crashed IT server. Insurance money will help pay for the PR campaign required to rebuild the reputation and other associated costs such as liability payouts or consequential legal fees. But these are different risks, not reputational risk. When it comes to reputational risk, prevention is the preferred option. The same applies for employee safety.

The concept of risk prevention is also a misnomer. You do not want to prevent risk completely as to achieve anything in business requires a certain amount of risk. To prevent a cruise liner sinking you would not go to sea. Rather the intent of risk management is to reduce risk in terms of frequency, likelihood, and consequence. That is, reduce the frequency of having to face the risk, the likelihood of the risk materialising and the impact to the business should it materialise.

The defences of self-insuring and transferring risk are predominately financial decisions and will not be discussed further.

Effective risk reduction comes from using an appropriate risk framework and relating it to the business processes and to the control points within the processes.

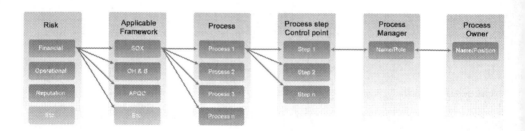

This model extends to reference the process manager and the process owner should these roles be different.

The importance of relating risk to process cannot be overstated. The definition of risk appetite is *"the nature and extent of risk a company is willing to take in order to meet its medium to long-term strategic objectives."* You have to take risks to be in business and the products and services of the business are delivered through the business processes. Therefore risk and business process can never be separated.

Organisational Learning:
It Takes Some Training

A factory owner was battling with productivity. He called in blue chip advisors to address the problem. They could not help. He called in specialist niche firms. They could not help. In desperation he called in a contractor he had been referred to. The contractor walked around the factory for ten minutes. He stopped at a machine and turned a screw one half turn. Productivity soared immediately. The delighted factory owner requested the invoice. It said, "Fee for addressing productivity issues—$20,000." The factory owner was astounded; $20,000 for 10 minutes work? He asked for an itemised invoice. It said, "Fee for turning screw—$5. Fee for knowing which screw to turn—$19,995."

It's an old story, but one I appreciate. It illustrates the difference between training and knowledge.

Individuals attend training and education sessions to develop their skills and knowledge. This raises the questions:

1. Can individually "owned" skill and knowledge be transferred to the organisation?
2. Can organisations learn in their own right?

I believe the answer to both these questions is yes, but the inputs and variables for organisational learning are different to those for individuals.

Broadly speaking (within the work context), individual learning has three inputs:

1. Company sponsored employee development programs
2. Participation in succession management programs
3. Personal development programs arranged by the employee.

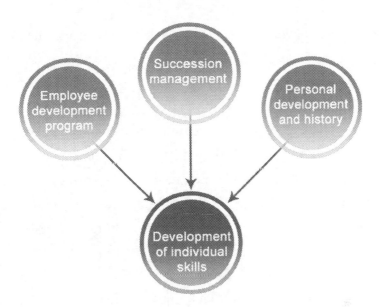

Employee development is the partner event to the performance appraisal. Typically an employee's performance is appraised annually and a development program is constructed to address weaknesses identified through the review. It is common that the development program is reviewed and refined quarterly while the performance review is held annually.

The intent of the development program is to build the skills of the individual. These can be technical, managerial, or soft skills.

Succession management is closely related to the employee development program but the time horizon can be five years out and succession management will consider and include additional organisational factors.

An important distinction is that organisations can have an employee development program without having a formal succession management plan, but not vice versa.

For the purposes of this article, personal development includes all other implicit or explicit learning an individual receives that makes them a better employee at work.

These three variables focus on the individual and collectively deliver a very talented individual—who could leave the company at any time. To minimise this risk, companies pour considerable sums of money into technology under the banner of "knowledge management." I support this approach but consider this knowledge capture, not organisational learning.

This distinction is not new. The ancient civilisations have always practiced it. Knowledge capture took the form of rock paintings and knowledge sharing took the form of storytelling. These stories were passed down from generation to generation and everyone knew them. This was true organisational learning.

Knowledge management in the form of technology and documentation will not be addressed in this article.

Organisational learning is the transfer of knowledge from the individual to the group through social interaction. You can transfer knowledge to a group, but you cannot transfer skills.

The most fundamental principle of organisational learning is that an organisation can only learn if it wants to.

When this is the case, an organisation will create time to learn. Creating time requires an organisation to stop "doing things" and start spending time to explicitly understand what and why they are doing what they do.

A key attribute of organisations is that they don't actually exist and this is particularly relevant when it comes to organisational learning. I say organisations don't exist as "organisation" is a collective noun for a group of individuals working together for a common purpose. As a collective, organisations can only learn through social interactions of which there are two primary types:

1. Projects
2. Business as usual.

Projects are where individuals come together to combine their individual learning to deliver an outcome that an individual could not easily deliver on their own. The project environment is by its nature a social environment.

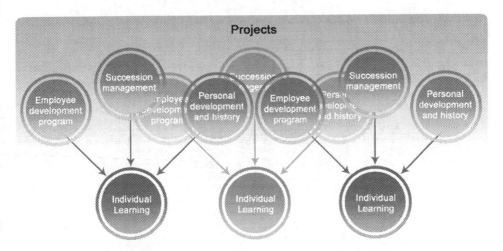

The project environment stimulates conversation and the sharing of ideas. It establishes a virtual bank of knowledge that represents the sum of all inputs. To stimulate learning, at the start of the project each member should present to the other team members as to how they will approach their responsibilities on the project. Then through the course of the project, each member should lead a discussion on lessons learnt to date. What has worked and what hasn't as compared to their original presentation. The principle is that you are always learning and while these lessons are fresh in your mind, you formally share them with the rest of the team. These discussions do not need to be long, but they should be formal and frequent. They represent the storytelling of the ancients. The audience can be restricted to the immediate group of business and project stakeholders.

This approach requires some additional project time. The project budget (time and cost) should allow for these sessions and the sponsor should accept the project will be delivered a week or two later than if you did not include these knowledge sharing activities.

If projects do not allow formal time for learning and the socialisation of the lessons, then the dissemination of knowledge is reduced to osmosis.

Business as usual differs from projects in that the social interactions are not as readily recognised as organisational learning opportunities.

The primary enabler for organisational learning in the business as usual environment is the organisational approach to governance. Effective governance is characterised by structured committees and the active management of variance.

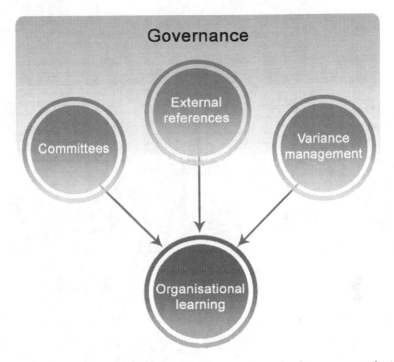

Committees are a group of individuals meeting to discuss agenda items. Within these meetings, time should be allowed to formally reflect on lessons learnt by the committee members over the last period. Depending on the committee, this reflection could happen only twice a year.

Variance management is the most important social interaction for organisational learning and its importance increases with seniority in the company. At the senior levels, business objectives can only be achieved through teamwork and managing variances is a team responsibility. As you move lower down the organisation variances can be attributed to individual managers or team leaders. Notwithstanding, a variance is an opportunity to explicitly consider what went wrong and what needs to change. When these conversations are seen as a learning opportunity then organisational learning is promoted.

The exchange of "lessons learnt" between the two social contexts becomes a knowledge multiplier.

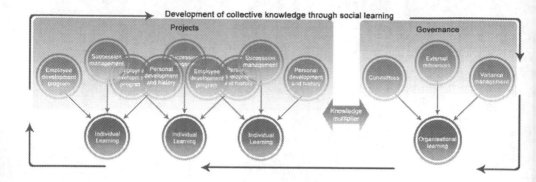

At the completion of the project, "lessons learnt" should be collated and formally presented to the wider stakeholder community. This will transfer knowledge to the widest group possible and help avoid a repeat of issues on the next project. Equally, those engaging in "business as usual" should formally present to project teams on their experience of the project and its business impact.

The organisational learning environment is maximised when the organisation formally recognises each component and the value in the interaction between them.

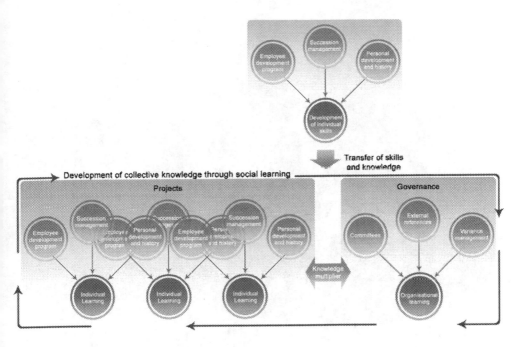

I am not suggesting that organisations learn randomly. The learning curriculum for an organisation is defined by its business strategy and the strength of the need to build the organisational capabilities necessary to deliver the strategy. Organisational capability is created by teams of people working together—the whole is greater than the sum of the parts. (I accept that technology plays an important part as well).

This hierarchy has a foundation on the knowledge and skills of individuals.

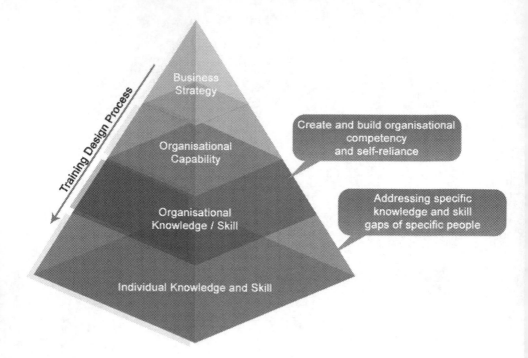

I close with a repetition of the most important aspect of organisational learning—organisations have to *want* to learn. If they do, then the above social events are the time to do it as they provide a consistent and enduring environment for active learning.